Mels Florence's

Book of Poetry

Melanie Lehtonen

AuthorHouse™
1663 Liberty Drive
Bloomington, IN 47403
www.authorhouse.com
Phone: 1 (800) 839-8640

Published by AuthorHouse   09/04/2018

ISBN: 978-1-5462-5621-2 (sc)
ISBN: 978-1-5462-5620-5 (e)

Library of Congress Control Number: 2018909810

Print information available on the last page.

authorHOUSE®

This book is dedicated to Jesus!

To her husband and children.

To her baby Bro Jared.

May God bless you all!

With love always!

Mels Florence

Melanie is a devoted Mother of five beautiful children.

She has two girls, Ashlynn 20 and Julianne 18.

She has three boys Dakota 16, Tristan 15,and Bryce 11.

Her Children are her pride and joy!

She has been married to her husband Derek for 19 years.

Melanie started writing poems at twelve years old.

Her joy of writing poems is evident!

She gives all glory to our Lord and Savior, Jesus Christ!

She is also a songwriter and loves to sing.

Melanie is the third oldest child from a family of ten.

Melanie is a positive person who loves to enjoy life to the fullest.

She loves the saying "Happiness is a choice!"

Besides spending time with her family, she likes gardening,

crocheting, cooking, hiking, and loves being outdoors.

In 2016 Melanie had a extensive brain surgery at Mayo Clinic in Jacksonville, Florida.

She has a brain condition called Chiari malformation and a syrinx.

She was born with this condition.

Mayfield Clinic Chiari center has a lot of information on this condition.

Please spread awareness!

She would like to say a special thanks to her family doctor, Dr. Edward Katemba

who helped her with getting the right treatment for her condition.

She thanks her Neurosurgeon Dr. Ronald Reimer and her Neurologist Dr. Benjamin Edelman.

She was in critical condition a few times.

She thanks her children for ALL the support they gave her.

She also thanks her Husband.

She would like to thank friends who helped.

Melanie has survived a lot in life including abuse.

She gives all glory to God!

Melanie hopes you enjoy her poems!!

These poems are about God, life, America, Abortion, bullying, etc....

To my baby,
I'll make this short and sweet!
To the man that makes my heart skip a beat.
Our love is strong and true.
Thank you for all you do.
Your still number one!
My heart is forever won.
I love you and I pray.
Big fish will come your way!
Love Mels

Don't ever think you're not loved.

Your my one and only sent from above!

If I could explain how special you are to me.

The words would go beyond much more than you could see!

If I let you down I am sorry and sad.

I know love is for the good.

And not to look on the bad!

You're not perfect, and neither am I!

So please don't be offended if I cry!

If I could show you my love always, I know.

That our love would always be strong and grow!

For the times I don't show you please keep loving me still.

Because I am trying to show you even if I am ill!

I always will love you and think the world of you.

My handsome husband with your eyes so blue!

You are my one and only.

And my love will always be true.

Love Mels

A Fisherman's Wife's Prayer

Bless him as he goes off today.

Keep him safe on the lake and on his way.

Help him to catch the fish, to win the tournament, that's my wish.

Let him give all glory to you.

That you are making his dream come true.

When the day is done, if he caught the fish or none.

Let him know he's still number one.

In his wife's eyes, he is the best!

The greatest catch of my life, I know I'm blessed!

Love

The truth about love.
It's sent from above!
It never seeks its own.
It starts with a stone.
When you make that promise to marry.
A strong love in your heart you carry!
Your eyes are filled with tears!
He kisses away your fears.
Your heart is so happy inside!
His love for you he'll never hide.
Your love for each other is so strong and true.
It's so beautiful, poetic, and you
can't wait to say I do!
With that ring you make a vow to marry.
It's a sacred vow in your heart, his
precious heart you carry!
Your lips and heart scream his name!
You know your life will never be the same!
Everything in you can't wait to be his bride.
You dream of the fairytale wedding and how
he'll kiss you makes you filled with pride.
You think nothing will break you
apart and you cherish his love!
Two hearts joined together from the deepest
parts of your souls binded, from above!

The truth about love is his strong arms
wrapped around you so tight!
His love will hold you through the night.
His kisses are warm, soft, gentle, and slow.
Every kiss makes your love grow!
The truth about love is don't take it for granted.
If you feel that love, it's truly by God planted!
Keep your vows so sacred and pure!
By your side he'll always be near.
Take that vow so seriously because a
broken shattered heart is something
you don't want to see!!
Hold that promise deep within your soul,
hold that love so happy and free.
The truth about love is he'll show his love and
it won't break if he meant it from his heart.
When you make that promise
seek God from the start!
If it's meant to be.
The whole world will see!!!!!
If we love one another his love is perfected in us.
In the book of John.
Love,Mels

Always a friend and loved
So beautiful
Helpful
Loving
You're strong
Nice
Never Alone

Joyful
Understanding
Loving
Incredible
Always loved
Nice
Never Alone
Everlasting

Defender
Awesome
Kind
Optimistic
Truthful
Always loved

Truly loved
Really awesome
Incredible
Smart
Trusting
Always strong
Nice

Baby
Really a miracle
You're loved
Caring
Excellent
Love Your Momma,
forever and always!!!!!

What would life be without each one of you?
You all cheer me up, that's what you do!
I've had no greater gift like you all in my life!
The miracles you are!
My love travels far!
I thank God and I can't thank him enough!
You my beautiful children have carried me when life gets tough!
Your treasures beyond anything I could have!
I wouldn't trade you for nothing!
I hope you always know .
That I will stand right by you whatever life may throw!
May God bless you and keep you and hold you everyday!
You are who I think of when I close my eyes to pray!
Your all so special and your loved more than you know!
I am so blessed and that will always show!
I want the best for you all!
I will pray God helps me when I fall.
I want to teach you all what matters in life!
That God died and saved you from all sin and strife!
He loves you and wants you to follow his way.
Till we all reach that glorious home in heaven someday.
Never let your love stop shining for him!
He is your Savior, redeemer, your friend!
God bless you as you grow and I will tell you again!
You are my miracles and my love will never end!!!!!
LOVE ALWAYS AND FOREVER! ~YOUR MOMMA ~

Another summer gone and school starts again!
Your Momma is crying tears and my heart aches within.
I pray you all have a good year!
And all know I hold you dear!
God bless you as you learn.
New pages of life to turn!
I pray you meet new friends.
And you'll be happy as the day ends!
I love you all and will miss you so much!
Always shine for Jesus and know he's never out of touch!
Love Always and forever!!!!! Your Momma

To My Children

My sweet babies that's what you'll be!
The joy I had within my heart when God gave you to me!
It was always my dream to be a mother.
The love I feel for you is like no other!
You're all so special in your own little way!
I love you all so much and this is what
I pray.
God bless my children and hold them close to you!
Help me be the best to them in all I say and do.
They are growing so fast!
The years are flying past!
Every moment let me treasure.
Let them know my love for them I cannot measure!
Bless their lives in every single way!
They are my gifts and the reason I'm so happy today!
Thank you God for their love!
It's only a miracle from above!!!!!
Love always, Your Momma

I don't want you to grow anymore!
I remember the day you were all three and four.
But yet you're all growing so fast!
As I watch you grow.
I want you all to know.
You're all so special to me!
I'm as proud as a Momma can be!
I couldn't be blessed more!
Each one of you I will always adore!
Always follow your dreams and heart.
I'm right beside you and have been from the start!
Wherever you go and whatever you do.
I will always love each and every one of you!
Love your Momma

I saw a homeless man today.
His clothes were ragged, his hair a disarray.
I wondered how he got to this point in life?
Had he ever had children or a wife?
Either way it made my heart sad.
I know I'm so blessed with all that I have.
As we Thank God for our blessings, this Thanksgiving day!
Let's remember to stop and help someone along the way!
Some people don't have a loving family, a warm home, or food to eat.
Let's pass our blessings on, to everyone we meet!
Love, Melanie Lehtonen
2017

Christmas

What is Christmas to you?
Is it a long list of things and you end up blue?
Is it how Christ came to live?
Or is it about how much you have to give?
Is it about spreading joy and cheer?
Or is it just another time of year?
Christmas is a time when all is happy and bright!
It is a time when our Savior was born on that cold night!
It's about showing love to those you hold dear!
It's about giving to those both far and near!
It's a time when we pray for peace!
It's a time when all fear should cease!
Christmas is a time to treasure!
It's a time when Christ came and his love you can't measure!
So let's remember the reason for this season and help a stranger!
It's about Jesus, his love, and how he was born in a manger!
Love, Mels

In God's eyes you're perfect and beautiful too!
You woke up this morning and the day is new!
Don't judge yourself or think of your battles within.
In God's eyes you're perfect and free from sin!
Don't let people bring you down, in God's eyes your
perfect, so don't be wearing a frown!
Think of his blessings and happy things too!
In God's eyes your perfect,
Smile no matter what the day brings you!
Live life to the fullest with love, hope, and peace!
In God's eyes your perfect,
His love for you will never cease!
Love, Mels

May your holy spirit lead me!
That is what I pray.
Help me be the best for you each and every day!
Lord I know I fail you, and don't always listen to your voice.
But you love me anyway and always give me a choice.
I can choose to follow you and take heed to your will.
Or I can disobey and make my life uphill!
Lord I know your ways are true.
That is what I want to do!
Help me be your servant.
I ask you now today!
To reach out to the hurting that come my way.
Give me love from above and give me strength to be!
The hands and feet of you Jesus that is what I plea!
Love, Mels

Breaking free from all the lies.
Made it hard to believe no matter how hard I tried!
I was so free when I realized it was for me he died!
I was scared and afraid and I thought I faced hell!
The preaching they preached never made me feel well.
I read in the bible of mercy, love and miracles taking place.
I read of God, Jesus and his saving grace!
How I should turn from sin and seek his face.
It wasn't a group of his chosen ones!!
He died for the whole world it was plain to see!
Not if you went to a church and told you should never leave.
I rarely felt love there only gossip if I fell!
It hurt so bad, but then they sin as well!
We are all sinners saved by his grace, he loves us no matter what we have done.
It's when we seek his forgiveness a new work has begun!
I want to shine for the world and tell Everyone!
There is hope and forgiveness in the risen Son!
No matter where you came from or what you have done.
In God's eyes your special and your number one!
Love Melanie Lehtonen

To write a list what we are thankful for!
God has blessed us with each other and so much more!
We are thankful for heat.
And the shoes on our feet.
We are thankful for food, so yummy to always fill our tummy!
We are thankful we are healthy and strong.
Also for good friends to help us along!
We are thankful for our home!
For a car to go wherever we roam.
We are thankful for the soldiers and that we are free!
We are thankful for our ears to hear and eyes to see!
Most of all I am thankful for me and Jesus!
He is always there to please us!
Love Mels

She tries to pretend that their words don't hurt.
But inside she's crying and she feels like dirt!
She put on her makeup and tried looking pretty today.
When she walked into school she wondered what they would say.
Lord be with me she prays.
But the taunting and laughing continues like in earlier days!
She tries to be nice and wants to fit in.
But they won't accept her and so it begins.
She questions is there something wrong with me?
When there is nothing wrong with her and she's pretty as can be!
She eats food to comfort her and cries when she's alone.
She goes to school everyday and can't wait to come home!
Parents teach your children how to treat others!
It's our duty as Fathers and Mothers!
To many kids are hurting and feeling alone.
Kids need to learn respect and that starts at home.
If someone's being bullied please know you are loved!!
God loves you, stand up and rise above!
Love, Mels

Lord I know she's far away.
But hold her close, this is what I pray!
Let her always feel your love.
Guide and keep her from above!
Bless her with health and good friends too.
And lift her up even if she is blue!
Give her peace through every trial.
Send rays of hope, joy, and a smile!
Bless her marriage and children too!
Lord, I know she is yours and that is what you will do!
Love, Mels

If I could go back today and change the things I have done!
I would have loved more often and leaned upon the Son.
The one who died and set me free!
Who gave his life on Calvary!
My God, my Savior you're the one I would have leaned upon!
I know I can't change the past or things I have done.
But I have hope, I am set free cause I leaned upon the Son.
The one who died to set me free!
Who gave his life on Calvary.
My God, my Savior you're the one I want to lean on.
Love Mels

To you that has suffered in pain.
If your tears are falling like rain.
If you're hurt has led you to addiction.
This is my conviction.
There is hope for you tonight.
Everything will be alright.
Only you and God know your pain.
And what you have been through.
Yet this is what he wants you to do.
Trust in him, there are better days ahead.
Ask him to forgive the life you have lead.
His peace and strength will carry you.
He will not forsake you and will help you through.
If you let go and trust in him.
Your days will be filled with gladness.
Jesus can take away your sadness.
Love, Mels

When you feel like no one cares.
He listens and he hears.
When your fears overtake you.
He says he won't forsake you.
When your hope is gone.
He says I will keep you strong!
When your tears won't stop falling.
Just remember, don't stop calling.
On the one who cares the most.
He is our God and Savior.
He is working in our favor.
He has a plan for you.
His words are always true!
There is hope in Jesus Christ.
It was for you he gave his life!
Psalm: When my heart is overwhelmed lead me to the rock that is higher than I.
Love, Mels

Hold on, be strong, that's what we have to do.

No matter how our life is and what we are going through.

Keep clinging to God's promises, and he will give you peace.

His love never fails and his blessings never cease!

Hold on, be strong, God has a plan for us all.

He is there to pick us up, and catch us if we fall.

He sends holy angels to watch over us every day.

He hears every sigh and listens when we pray!

Hold on, be strong, he'll wipe away our tears.

He knows our thoughts and all your fears.

He will give us strength for every trial we go through.

Just hold on be strong, that's what we have to do!

Love, Mels

Letting go of the hurt and pain.
Feelings coming from the heart, tears falling like rain.
You have chosen to forgive.
To walk in joy and happily live.
The feelings of anger you held on to so long.
Are all gone now, and in your heart is a new song!
You still may not understand why or have all the answers.
To why they hurt you or made you cry.
Being bitter only hurts and destroys you.
Takes the happiness and joy from your life.
No matter what you do.
The freedom you feel when you forgive!
The peace you have, it's the way to live.
Love, Mels

When I think of how you died, left bleeding and crucified.
I tremble from within, knowing that it was also for my sin.
To think you died for us all!
For all sin great or small.
That you were nailed to the cross, so no soul would be lost.
My tears fall down with joy and praise!!
You rose in just three days!
You set us free, with your blood stains.
Your love for us, to this day remains!
Thank you Jesus for dying for me, for remembering me at Calvary!
Love, Mels

I look to the sky and I see your love!
It's in the moon, stars, and sun above!
I see the beauty and glory in the skies.
So often it's brought tears to my eyes.
The moon is a glow like I need in my heart.
To shine for others, to see your love, that will never part!
The stars twinkle so magnificent for me.
To know the many blessings you give.
To show others you're light, and for you we should live.
The sun is warm and a reminder for me.
That you sent your Son to die for me!
When I look to the heavens above, I see your glory always!
Sometimes the sky is stormy all clouds in sight.
That's for me to know that it's sometimes a struggle and many trials.
But your light and your love is behind those clouds!
Waiting for me to cry up to you.
You hear me always and answer me.
My child I'm with you, it will be alright soon!
I'll take you to the heaven of heavens, far more wonderful than you can see.
Seek me first and come to me.
And I promise you'll have eternity!!
Love, Melanie

Warm sweat drips from his brow, as he picks up his gun!
His body is tired but the day has just begun!
Lord give me strength he softly prays.
He thinks of his family, he hasn't seen in days!
The picture of his baby, brings tears.
I wonder if I'll see her again, he fears.
He wonders if he made the right choice coming here.
The place where danger is so near.
Then he stops and he remembers….
Once again he stands tall!
America is free and it's worth it all!
He's an American soldier you see.
He's the reason we are all free.
He risks his life for you and me!
Let's remember him on bended knee!
Love, Melanie Lehtonen

Unborn baby, don't you cry!
God never wanted you to die!
He had a plan for your precious life.
Satan took it away and made it seem right.
Some Mommy's arms longed to hold you tight.
To comfort you when you cried at night.
Your body was perfect and beautifully formed.
Your Mommy probably loved you, she was just misinformed.
She feels guilt now and dreams about you.
The horror she felt when you came out blue!
God forgives your Mommy but now she can't go back.
She could have given you away, and gotten her life back on track.
Unborn baby, don't you cry!
God never wanted you to die!!
You are one of the many angels above.
Some Mommy wanted you to have and to be loved!
Rest with Jesus, now you are safe!
Now he is kissing your beautiful face!
Love, Mels

She sees it on the internet, in the magazines and on tv.
All the perfect bodies.
And wishes that could be me!
She looks at all the ads.
The famous trends and fads.
She wants to be that pretty and thin.
Then a voice comes from within.
Beauty is within the heart!
God wants you to be you, and this is how to start!
He said you are fearfully and wonderfully made.
Don't look at the fads that will slowly fade.
Your body is perfect from the creators hand.
He needs you to reach out to this lost and lonely land!
To use your talents that he only gave!
To reach out to lost that God came to save!
Help those in need.
Shine for Christ and to his words heed!
For men shall be lovers of themselves from which turn away.
Let us be beautiful, in a Godly way!
Love, Mels

In Memory of (9/11) attack on America

I will never forget that day thirteen years ago.
How I felt when I saw those planes flying low.
It made my heart stop and skip a beat as tears started to flow!
I prayed for our country and the innocent lives lost, that thirteen years ago.
I remember clinging tight to my husband and children that quiet September night.
I remember praying to God that our country would be alright!
My first born Son was in my belly and due in about a month.
I thought of all the Mommy's and Daddy's
that lost their children.
All because of someone's evil stunt!!!
Let us never forget September 11th, and the tragedy that took place!
Let us remember who we turned to, when the towers turned to waste!
America is still standing, and our country is still free.
Dear God bless America and help us to see!
That we need to go back, like in earlier days when we prayed in the schools.
When we said in God we trust!
This is a must!
Let us shine for all!
Once again stand tall!
God bless the land of the free!!
Love, Mels Florence

Whoever slanders his neighbor in secret him will I put to
silence, is what the good book says. Psalm 101
Gossip spreads like fire and the tongue is hard to tame.
If we are doing this to our brother let us hang our heads in shame!
God wants us to be loving, reaching out to those that fall.
For us to judge and talk about them is not our duty at all!
No matter what they are doing or what they have done.
There is grace and forgiveness in the risen Son!
So before we judge somebody, let's try walking in their shoes!
Not be the first to gossip and spread the latest news!
Let's have a Christian like heart and show love to everyone!
Our love, compassion, and prayers might just change someone!
Love, Mels

CHIARI MALFORMATION

God knows he's here.
Nothing to fear.
You won't fall down.
If you do you'll have a crown.
Don't cry beautiful girl!
God is always with you, for real!
When you are weak, you will be made strong!
Even when the journey has been long!
Five years and still counting.
You're a fighter, let your tears fall like a fountain!

CHIARI STRONG
Melanie Lehtonen

I smile like nothing's wrong.
But inside I am fighting and trying hard to hold on!
I wake up thanking God for another day.
I ask for strength as I pray.
God help my balance today!
I can hardly walk and I sway.
Love, Mels

Waiting for answers can be so hard!
I try be strong, but I feel so weak.
Lord help me listen when you speak.
Living in pain.
Lord don't let me complain.
You have promised strength for the day!
And help along the way!
I am trying so hard and help me if I cry.
I know you promise that every tear you'll dry!
God, I'm begging you tonight.
Please heal me, and tell me everything is going to be alright.
I know in heaven we will have no pain.
But here on earth there is sickness and
there is healing in your name.
I take all my sickness to you!
God I know you will take my sickness and
heal me through and through!
Mark in the bible Ch 16 verse 18 .
And they shall lay hands on the sick and they will recover!
Amen your word says it.
The Lord will give strength unto his people!
I love you!
Love, Mels

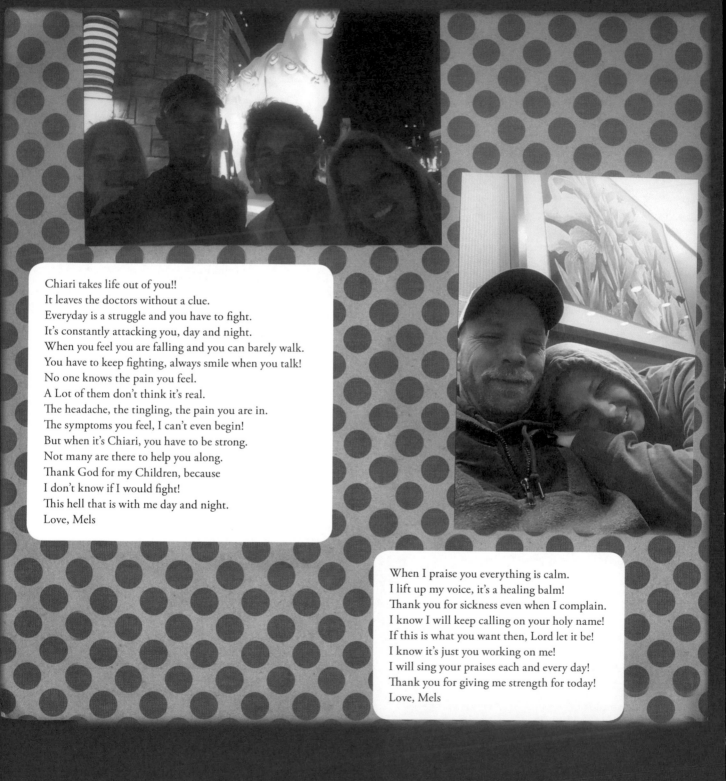

Chiari takes life out of you!!
It leaves the doctors without a clue.
Everyday is a struggle and you have to fight.
It's constantly attacking you, day and night.
When you feel you are falling and you can barely walk.
You have to keep fighting, always smile when you talk!
No one knows the pain you feel.
A Lot of them don't think it's real.
The headache, the tingling, the pain you are in.
The symptoms you feel, I can't even begin!
But when it's Chiari, you have to be strong.
Not many are there to help you along.
Thank God for my Children, because
I don't know if I would fight!
This hell that is with me day and night.
Love, Mels

When I praise you everything is calm.
I lift up my voice, it's a healing balm!
Thank you for sickness even when I complain.
I know I will keep calling on your holy name!
If this is what you want then, Lord let it be!
I know it's just you working on me!
I will sing your praises each and every day!
Thank you for giving me strength for today!
Love, Mels

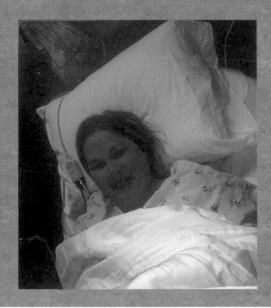

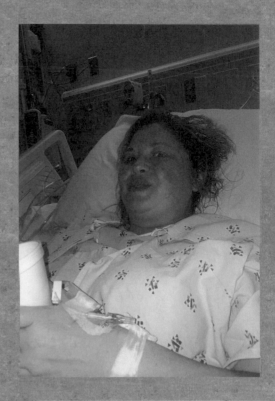

Heal me from sickness oh Lord, I pray!
I want to watch my kids, to be there everyday!
My pain hurts so bad.
Sometimes it makes me mad.
Please Lord it's more than I can bare!
My feet, my legs, Lord you know every tear.
I want to be joyful and not complain.
But Lord I can't handle the pain.
My husband sees it and I don't want
to cry and tell him I hurt.
Please Lord, give me back my health.
It's worth more than wealth.
Help me not complain.
Help me bear the pain.
I know the sun shines after the rain.

I want to shine for you, to
be a good mother and wife
and be there for others!
Thank you Lord for
hearing me now.
I love you and please give
a good day tomorrow!
Love always! Mels

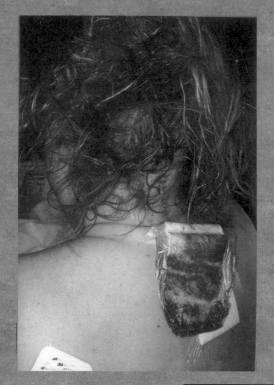

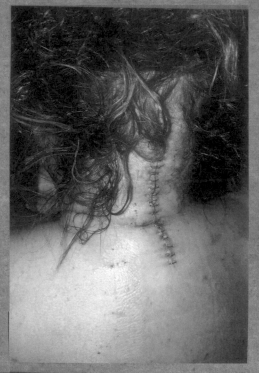

Tomorrow is not promised
to me or to you.
Let's shine for the world
in all that we do!
Let's love and laugh
with all our hearts.
Forgive one another
as each day starts!
Let's let go of all anger,
bitterness, and fear!
Let's make changes, take chances
cause we only live a while.
Let's live each day to the fullest
with a happy heart and a smile!
Love, Mels

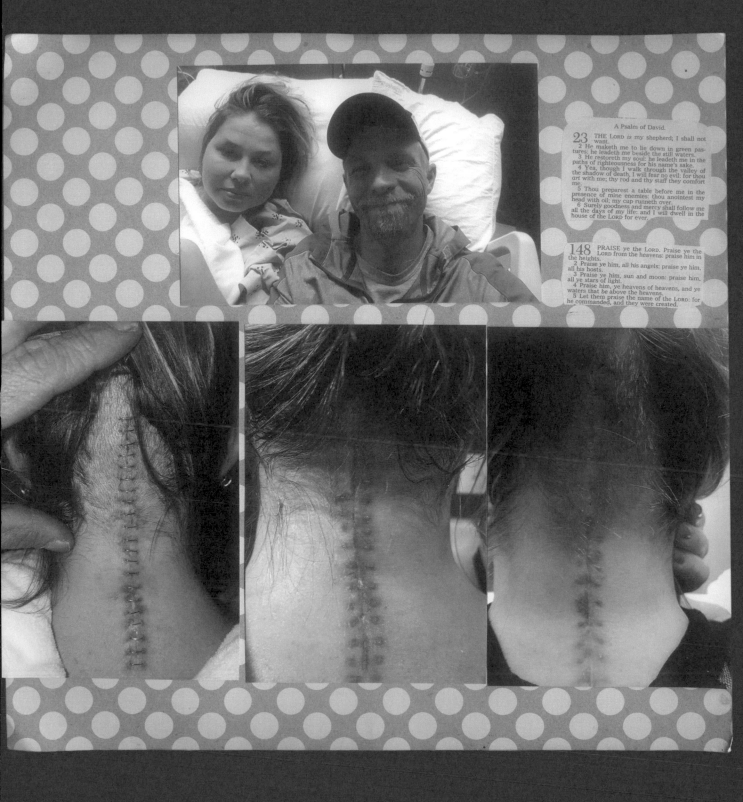

Printed in the United States
By Bookmasters